Zim's Foolish History of Horseheads
By Eugene Zimmerman, 1911
Restored and reprinted by New York History Review, 2021
Elmira, New York

For information on getting permission for reprints and ex-
cerpts, contact us through our website:
www.NewYorkHistoryReview.com

ISBN: 978-1-950822-17-1

First edition
Printed in the United States of America

Original cover drawing by Eugene Zimmerman.

Eugene Zimmerman

Conceit is world-wide, when a man accomplishes something or other he wants the world to know just how wise and brainy he looks, no matter even if he looks like ——? One man will deliberately saturate his system with some sort of patent medicine for the sake of witnessing his own picture and testimonial in a "Ready Relief" pamphlet, while another will deface a handsome cigar label with his homely countenance, or a $3.50 pair of shoes of his own make. But how much does it interest the public what sort of an ape made this or that brand of talcum powder or gooseberry shaving soap so long as the article is of quality and does the work it is calculated for?

At the earnest solicitation of my printer and publisher and greatly against my personal wishes I append my portrait to this volume and trust you will forgive me for doing so.

The original design for this statue called for a white man's scalp instead of the bunch of hemlock cigars, but that was while the battle was on and bets were being offered 10 to 1 on "Red Jacket." The moment the Western Union wires announced the defeat of the Chief and his tribe of noble red men he became a slave to the cigar trade. Thus the bunch of wooden cigars which you see in this picture became the true emblem of that noted conquest.

This book is most respectfully dedicated to the loving memory of my late dog Patsy, who met his doom while attempting to wreck a trolley car.

Tried and true was he and homely as a hedge fence, also honorary member of many dog societies of the neighbrhood.

Half mourned, half damned, a dash hound in every sense of the word; had many dash————— it—te—dashes ahead of his name and would answer as readily to any alias in the vocabulary of profanity as to the humble name Patsy.

But alas he is no more, may his soul rest in pieces.

MORAL—''T'was better so, however, than into sausage links.''   —The Author.

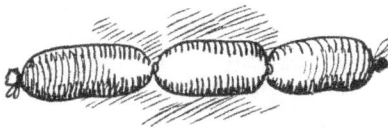

This is a great grandson of the first settler,whom we have retained to impart the story of the origin of the name "Horseheads" to strangers who have the time and inclination to stop and listen. History gives us the story in many blood curdling lines, but this gentleman has repeated it so often that he is now able to confine it to a few words, thusly:

"More than a hundred years ago, General Sullivan come throo here and cleaned out the injuns and after he got throo with 'em,they wasn't nuthin left but a pile o' horses he'ds. So our great grandfathers held a pow-wow and decided to call it Horseheads and went right to work and built a still and continued drinking corn whiskey where the injun left off. Don't know what'd a become of us if they'd found a pile of horse tails instead. Anyhow they didn't and that's why sich is the case.

After establishing Horseheads and driving a stake to indicate where Pritchard Hall was to be erected and that all future county conventions should prevail at that point he (Sullivan) took a liberal chaw of John I. Nicks, and ordered his troops to beat it for the Chemung River where his naval forces were concentrated. Having finished the great work of his life in establishing Horseheads, he ordered his gun boats and ox teams to proceed down the river (one by land, the other by water) as far as Wellsburg, N. Y., where a site was selected and contracts let for the erection (in future years) of a monument to commemorate his unwelcome visit to the Indians. Being quite familiar with the treacherous Chemung river and the possibility of having his cherished hobby (the monument) washed down to Waverly on a June flood, he was particularly careful in selecting a site with some elevation to it, where now stands the pile of stone, which recalls to our mind one hot afternoon in 1879 when we attended the dedication exercises and paid five cents a glass for water to chase down the contents of our pocket flask. It would be well for future warriors who anticipate the building of monuments to their memory, to use this sad instance as an object lesson and advise in their anti mortem statement the erection of such in closer proximity to a licensed hotel.

"Bah!" ejaculated General Sullivan, "I'm the landlord here now. You get thy rusty ole traps together and skiddoo. I want to change the name o' this place to Horseheads, N. Y.

As we cuddle around the little dingy forge at the blacksmith shop, adding a squirt of tobacco juice here and there (our daily tribute for the kindness bestowed on us by the blacksmith) little do we realize the extent of our importance upon this great sphere—how necessary it is that we be

here to shoulder our share of the burden. Horse-heads is but a speck on the map, though it occupies just as much space on said map as any other, (fly-specks barred of course.) Yet some of these specks, representing cities of many thousands of inhabitants, are much larger in extent than our town, and spend millions (?) of dollars annually in publicity advertising which seldom yields any substantial return. Promoters seem to overlook the importance of special features to draw attention to their fair city. They point out their superb shipping facilities, lay great stress on their perfect school system and perhaps put in a good word for the excellent cusine of the jail.

Now, we do not wish to brag about our own booming propensities or our originality when we start in to pull off a stunt, but, dear reader, before you spend any money for publicity work, send your press agent to us for advice. Horseheads

never does a thing half way, it doesn't know
enough to quit there. It goes the full limit; for instance: Last year—to break the monotony—
Horseheads gave its citizens a Post Office Hold-up
The audience was small and unappreciative we
must admit, but as the yeggmen neglected to
properly advertise their presence in town, and, we
being a peaceable people, the town naturally went
into repose early. However, the episode proved
such a colossal success in point of advertising that
our Chamber of Commerce decided to arrange with
Safe Crackers (of the highest type) for an annual
holiday hold-up, turning Hanover Square into a
vast arena with seats at all points of vantage,
properly shielded and protected with ''Harvey-
ized'' steel armor plates and electrical spot lights
to lessen the labors of the actors—the gate re-
ceipts will be devoted to making good the losses

sustained by the Post Master and postal authorities and let us add that the Zim Band will furnish
the music.

The E. W. L. & R. R. Co. will co-operate with us
so far as car service and spot light effects is con-

cerned and a special (double) seat will be erected for Supt. Mr. Fran Maloney.

The foregoing episode was but a trifling matter yet it caused the newspapers of the world to print the name, Horseheads, N. Y. Some even went so far as to use red ink. When you do something which makes the big dailies "sit up and take notice" in large red headlines, a feeling of Dr. Cookism takes possession of you, and you are liable to become chesty. But, not so with us; we conduct our little sensations quietly, peacefully and without gusto—and if we are able to bring about certain conditions we will have no further use for a police department.

There is one advantage at least in having the postoffice robbed once a year. We get rid of our shelfworn stock of stamps, the gum on whose back has become so flavorless that it is no longer a luxury to lick them.

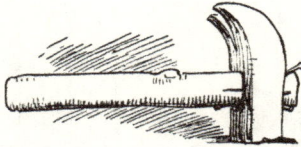

An unpopular implement still used by various inhabitants in a favorite pastime known as knocking.

Yes indeed stranger! Time was when every able bodied galoot of us had to bend our masculine spine and help drag the old three ton fire engine to the handiest watering trough. Fire fighting nowadays seems more like picnicing, for we rely solely upon the strong arm and happy disposition of our

Superintendent of water works to man the emergency pump at a moment's call and do the work formerly accomplished by our fossil fire engine.

Note here the superintendent in question has just received a phone call to replenish the reservoir. Note also the happy and contented expression of his western exposure, for in this picture he

is facing the east. Doesn't he look as if he was thoroughly satisfied with his job? "Well I guess" —and right he should be for he gets more than any other mortal in the municipal service and just as many cusses besides. I forgot to state that the square object in his port side hip pocket is a chunck of navy plug (of the old school variety) with the corner bit off. A man displaying such personal economy is certainly entitled to the good will and support of the voters, regardless of creed or color.

Alderman Mark Taber who spends his evenings with the bosom of his family. "Mark" is a great dog fancier. This picture shows him wending his

way homeward after a board meeting, with his little Frankforts, the pride of his kennel and his little tin companion filled with some sort of fluffy stuff.

We will now take up fire matters.

We maintain an expensive Fire Department for the sole purpose of holding fairs. It consists of one four wheel Chemical, one Hook & Ladder, three Hose Carts, one Crippled Engine, one Supply Wagon and two bushels of Soft Coal—besides this we have about half a million gallons of pure Spring Water, carefully wrapped in concrete, upon a hill of sufficient height to develop a pressure of ninety lbs. to the inch (Whatever that means?)

In spite of this elegant and efficient equipment we are almost fireless. To the lovers of fire excitement Horseheads is an uninteresting place, for they are too few and far between. Ask any old citizen when the last fire occurred and he'll

scratch his head and think and think, and you go
on your way leaving him scratching and thinking.

Next under the hammer is our fire alarm which
is a peacharino. It consists of a real bell hung
in the cupola of a structure of modern architecture
known as the Fire Headquarters, which in truth it
is.   The bell is soft in tone and as its peal flits
through the night's stilly air, one feels that the
millennium has come. It seems to say, ''Put on
your pants and get out! Put on your pants and
get out!''—and when you are out and on the

street you discover that you have left off your collar and necktie, so you go back, of course, and make your toilet properly. By this time the fire has had time to develop a red glow which acts as a beacon light and you can readily see in which direction to run.

There is one case on record where the telephone (night) operator phoned to the Elmira Light Co. please to turn on the lights so the firemen can find the fire.

Every year a new Chief is elected. His duties are to wear the only white helmet in the department and carry a german silver fog-horn with bright red tassels appended (and filled with gaudy posies) on Annual Parade Day. He also wears the suit of his predecessor in office which usually fits like the proverbial ''Paper on de wall.'' He is permitted to offer suggestions as to the manner of fighting fires. However, as the rest of the department is made up of former chiefs and ex-officers, everybody gives everybody else orders and everything goes.

When I began this truthful narrative I fully intended letting the printing contract to one Edward Riker, who used to be boss printer and general manager of the old ''Horseheads Journal,'' a Greenbacker and when that sheet became defunct, ''Ed'' received the bulk of its outfit in settlement of some back salary.

Sad to relate, I discovered that he was using wooden shoe pegs in his make up, in place of solid lead type. I, therefore, relieved him of the responsibility and set him to mowing the lawn and doing other chores about my premises wherein he fits to my utmost satisfaction.

The matter is now in the hands of Geo. Mulford, our able and versatile editor of the Chemung Valley Reporter.

George is the man who sadly remarked in an overcrowded issue of his paper that owing to lack of space this week, many births and deaths have been postponed. In its palmiest days the "Texas Siftings" never had one to beat this.

I have retained this remarkable student of Blackstone to settle all libel suits that may arise from the publication of family secrets.

Anybody wishing to start a legal scrap will please notify this gentleman of their intentions.

Let it be known that Frank Armitage has graft-ed a choice variety of grapes into his bean vines and will hereafter devote his spare time to his half acre vineyard. The grapes are to be used in the manufacture of "Great Western Champagne" (that celebrated exhilerator) without which no well regulated household is complete.

OUR MOTTO: "What is home without Great Western?"

There is no doubt about it that Horseheads was originally selected as the most suitable site for the Garden of Eden, but for some slight misunder-standing on the part of those who had the matter in charge evidently things got mixed on their maps for here we had all the required stage settings for this beautiful drama—the snakes, the apple trees, the balmy atmosphere, in fact every detail but the fig leaf, and (if we are to take any stock in bible history) that brief foliage didn't cut much ice, a bunch of corn husks would have been just as comfortable and attractive, as quality or quantity in garments in those days was a secondary consideration. There were no key-holes nor opera glasses nor inquisitive neighbors in the Garden of Eden, so what was the use of putting on unnecessary airs, but as I said before they got mixed and skipped us.

Thus the Garden of Eden was planted elsewhere and we began to look forward to the time when General Sullivan would do his Indian killing act. Time brought this about and here we are handing it to you right off the griddle, just as our great grandmother told it to our grandmothers, and our grandmothers told it to our mothers, and our beloved mothers told it to us.

Note the expression on the fellow behind the bass drum. This is the Zim Band. The picture is true to life in every detail, though on this particular occasion there happened to be a prize fight billed in Elmira, therefore, but seven of its most earnest workers appear on the scene above. It is necessary to maintain a body of twenty-five soloists in order to get a full band of seven pieces for any special purpose and often at rehearsals you will find just the bass drummer and the leader present. However, as the bass drum is about the only instrument always out of tune, we don't wonder that the bulk of the band preferred the prize fight.

The band is a great acquisition to our town. You bet, it puts ginger into us, causes us to step lively and sets our patriotic blood to coursing. So if you love music you can find it at least one night a week in Teal Park. Come up and shake hands with your rube cousins.

Our "Village Board" is made up of five worthies (nominated against their will) who have no axes to grind. At some time or other nearly every adult has served in that capacity, so you can judge we have many worthies and ex-worthies in our community.

The President of the Board is elected by a vote of the people and without the use of a blooming coin and most always succeeds himself and continues to ditto until he can find another willing soul to relieve him of the honor.

It is necessary to have a particularly handsome man at the head of our village government, thus, for his superior qualifications, marked beauty and manly grace, Collins Hathaway was handed the lemon. He is now on his second lap and still bears up well and from outward appearance and public

expression he will (or rather must) endure in-
definitely.

The office is without compensation whatever, so
we cannot say that "graft" lured him from the

narrow path. A man accepting this honor does it
with the full knowledge that he is entering martyr-
dom, for to him come many kicks and cusses. Be-
lieve me, every mother's son who has ever served
on the Board should be permitted to wear a golden
crown forever thereafter.

Of course there is hardly a political office on top
of this earth that has not some perquisite attach-
ed. So it is in the case of our trustee. He gets
a little "rake off" now and then in the way of
worn out top dressing and rubbish off the streets.
If he has a vacant lot which needs filling in, he is
at liberty to help himself. I was on the Board
two years, when I began my term my lot was
very uneven in spots, but mind you, when my
term expired the same lot was as level as a
parlor floor. In this way we have been able to put

our village (which used to be so full of pit falls
and irregularities) on the level—taking it from
one place to put in another until we are all on the
level.—(I said all on the level.)

A true picture of the interior of Police Headquarters, including the Chief, after an arduous
day of police duty. The unsympathetic stranger
not thoroughly acquainted with all the circum-
stances connected with this officer's life would
deem him shiftless and lazy, but mind you, he per-
forms many other duties during each twenty-four
hours—for besides Chief of Police, he is the whole
Police Department, Assistant Deputy Sheriff, Janitor of the Jail, rocks the baby to sleep and carries up coal for his mother. Therefore I beg of
you, do not misjudge this man should he seek to

acquire the 40 winks to which each mortal is
entitled.

BURNS.   DRAKE   UPDIKE,   PLATT

Our four hotel landlords declaring under oath that they do not adulterate their respective beverages—never did and never shall.

P. S.—It was discovered, however, that the Court Bible was at the cobbler's shop being half soled and a Webster Dictionary substituted in its place, and besides the left hand was used in making the solemn declaration, therefore, it will not stand in the community where these gentlemen are known.

※ ※ ※ ※ ※

Jonas Van Duzer requires no formal introduction as he has lived among us always. He frequents the same haunts and occupies the same pew in life's drama as we and us. Jonas can point out to you the virtues of Buttermilk, its hip reducing qualities and general health replenishing properties. He learned much in this respect by way of the reknown Dr. Flynn, the Buttermilk lecturer, during his sojourn in Elmira.

Mr. Van Duzer has a beautiful and commodious

homestead situated on the west bank of Newtown Creek (when the tide is out) and on all sides when the tide is in; a sort of floating farm as it were. He plants cabbages above the R. R. bridge and plucks them below (yea, many miles below). For years Jonas has paid taxes on land belonging to his neighbor above him, which the creek deposited during one of its sprees in Jonas' back yard, but Mr. Van is not a man to kick or growl but goes right ahead cultivating each year, the land of said neighbor which is left at his doorstep by said Spring flood.

Jonas builds his pigstys on pontoons and anchors them to his apple trees, which is another point in his favor as a progressive agriculturalist.

The creek gets very familiar at times; it steps right up to his dining room table without even so much as an invitation. It has cost the state a considerable sum to settle with Jonas for its fresh-

ness and it served it right. The state should teach this naughty stream better manners and not allow it to leave its bed at will to roam about the neighborhood.

A Hustling Scene on a Saturday A. M. at the First National.   John Bennett, Banker.

The faithful watch dog of our 30 day notes, Owner and Proprietor of the Money Repository of Horseheads.   This man has such a pull with the Government that he is able to purchase greenbacks by the yard, sign his name to them, cut them up in strips and retail them at one hundred cents on the dollar.

One of the largest and most extensive industries is the Horseheads Creamery Company. Its product spreads over the bread of many states. It has three distinct heads—Jonas Van Duzer, Sayre Holbert and Oliver Eisenhart, all working in unison for one

common cause ($).   Three of a kind as it were.
All aces.

This combination owns and operates about a
dozen creameries in other parts of this State and
Pennsylvania.   Its financial base is Horseheads.
Here's where we "rake off" for the "Kitty" and
divide the pot.

Their specialty is conveying lacteal fluid into
butter, skim milk into cheese, whey into curd, and
curd into paper sizing and pants buttons.

Every package bears their signature.   None
genuine without it.

The first, last and only picture of Big Chief
"What's-His-Name" urging his what-is-it against
Sullivan's troops.   At this exciting moment the
"Big Chief" went into posterity, as did also the
nag.

Foot Note—I wish to add by way of an editor's
foot note that in those days they used no bridles.
Horses were taught a code of signals by a pressure

on their wind pipe.   The signal in the said picture means "Go-it-Gallagher!"

As we are only interested in Horseheads I have
omitted the other end of the animal.

"Hello! Hell-O! Central!
This is Dr. Stork—S-T-O-R-K—Yes!   The young
  Dr.
Give me Ollie Eisenhart.
"Hello Ollie, is that you?"
"Want anything in my line this year?   Got a full
assortment of singles, doubles and triplets, both
sexes in pink and red tints.   I can match up any-
thing you have in stock with pug or hook noses.
Don't forget to order early, Old Boy."

A favorite pastime open to every man, woman
and child is our Spring sucker fishing.   When the
creek is up and roily one sees the curtains drawn
and doors bolted at our various places of business,
which indicates that suckers are running.   The
bank of the stream presents a picture such as no
artist could (or would) paint.   There the hostler
and the artisan are on an equal plain, both baiting
the same sort of hooks with the same sort of
worms and setting in the same sticky mud which
is so profuse on its banks in the Spring of the year.
But the joy, the utter abandon which one exper-
iences and the many ailments one can accumulate

on one of these trips is beyond description. One must be on the spot to appreciate it. Come and try it and by so doing give your family doctor a chance to earn an honest living.

LIN GARDNER.

"Go-lang there, gol darn yer!" muttered he in audible tones. "Can't yer see it's near time for George's paper to go ter press?"

"Lin" Gardner hurrying to press with his sassy weekly personal. (With apologies to Lin, likewise the mules.)

P. S. Further comment is unnecessary I assure you, having had one experience with this able writer and ensilage chopper I prefer to remain quiet.

By the way, I will vary the subject by telling you a little story about Dr. Bush. There is an old saying that "a baby is born at every tick of the clock," but in the case of Dr. Bush one might say there's a soul born whenever Doc sits down to play cards, for it is gospel truth that whenever the Doctor gets down to a card game, be it whist, cribbage, hearts, binocle or poker, he is sure to leave the game unfinished to answer a call to Sullivanville and Doc true to his professional instincts has

left many a stack of chips in the center of the
table and laid down the winning hand to serve one
in distress.

Doc is a hero in every sense of the word and
richly deserves the support of the young demo-
crats who twenty or forty years ago were given
their first dose of paragoric by the hand of Dr.
Bush. I am inspired to offer the following heroic
effusion which I will permit to be chisled upon a
suitable tablet and placed in the center of our
village.

"On! On! to Sullivanville" commanded the
Major, as he thrust his rusty saber into the busty
rubber flanks of his trusty gasoline steed, "For
who knows but ere the morning breaks another
soul shall be added to swell the Democratic ranks
of our commonwealth."

The portraits in this book were made largely
from memory (which I carry with me on certain
occasions and which I might have overstretched in
some cases.) I struggled to give a faithful repro-
duction of each and every individual and their
short-comings, also their good qualities, but never
have I stuck my nose into their business. I trust
therefore that you will handle me lightly when
called upon to criticize this work.

Jerome Platt, proprietor of the celebrated Platt House, was the first landlord to recognize the need of steam heat to make his guests comfortable during the cold winter nights. We give here an illustration of Jerome's ingenuity of installing an individual steam plant in each room. This method enabled him to advertise his house as the only hotel heated by steam. The system has been much improved since.

A Word to the Tramp by L. M. Brown, Police Justice.

We have a most kindly disposed police force to take you in, also an hospitable poor master to cater to your tastes. Our jail is roomy and airy and handsomely whitewashed. Its latchstring is always out. When you happen our way drop in and stay a day or two. I bid thee welcome.

HOT SHOTS.

Horseheads is the political pivot of Chemung County and Pritchard Hall the birth place of many an illustrious political career.

For more than half a century its inner walls have withstood the bombardment of eloquent oratory and the hot air frequently dispensed, to no avail, has loosened the plaster in many spots to an alarming degree.

Our conventions are what we might call a Mingling of "Cheerful Spirits."

Many a candidate has slipped into office while the deciding vote was out having its throat sprayed.

The throat sprayers got wise to the fact a year ago that it would be better to tolerate a little hoarseness than to allow the water wagons to monopolize the entire road—so they remained around the polls. Well, you know the rest.

Smoke the "ZIM" Cigar. A hero medal presented with every box. They are made by a big gun by the name of Cannon. He assumes all risks so I feel safe in recommending them to the

most cultivated tastes. We have further the
assurance of its maker of the sterling worth of
this delicate article bearing our name. Try one
and "May the Lord have mercy upon your soul."

**Hon. Rho L. Bush, Guardian of the Village
Exchequer.**

This pictures that trusty officer in the act of depositing into the village safe deposit vaults the
sum of three dollars and sixty-five cents (all
nickels) which was handed in by a delinquent tax
payer at the time our camera was in action.

THE OLD CANAL.

Where once flowed the Chemung Canal there is
but an impression in the mud, with a spring of
pure, sparkling water gurgling here and there,
garnished with crisp water-cress.

The canal was a great feature in its day, and
like all good things, it outlived its usefulness and
was obliged to take a seat among the has-beens.
Nevertheless we love to recall those boyhood days
when she was in her maiden bloom and we bathed
in her bosom, yes, our soul filled with joy and our
mouths and ears with bull-heads and dead clams.
Ah me! **Maybe them wan't great days!** And to

think that there is nothing left to remind us of them, except, perhaps, the Chemung Canal Trust Company which bears its honored name. And particularly if you happen to have paper there overdue.

I forgot to inquire whether the canal was built before Sullivan slew the Indians, but I think not. It is my honest impression that it happened a few years later. At any rate we mustn't forget that it did exist, flourish and furnished valuable material for this book.

Exclusive High Sign recently adopted by the Horseheads "Blue" lodge. "Eastern Star" members are forbidden to use this without a written permission.

Noticeable Symptoms of Temporary Insanity.

When one insists on telling a funny story while the host says grace.

When one eats soup with his fork.

And sponge cake with his spoon.

Picks his teeth with his index finger.

Blows his nose on his napkin.

Wipes his mouth on the table cloth.

And laps up the lemonade in the fingerbowl.

EUGENE VAN NAME.

We are also indebted to the Lane Bridge Company of Painted Post, N. Y., for the money it has unconsciously placed at our disposal. Gene Van Name, its hustling salesman, is an enterprising citizen of Horseheads and much of the coin which finds its way into the channel of commerce bears the stamp of the aforesaid company and is put in circulation by our townsman.

Mr. Van is full of energy, "gimp and git'thar." Sunrise finds him up and warbling with the birds, for Gene has a tenor that mingles well with the morning's pure ozone.

This trophy was handed him by a neighbor over the back fence at a distance of forty feet as a mark of appreciation of his morning carol.

AN INFALLIBLE RECEIPT.

For those who wish to prolong life 1,000 years.
NEVER worry about your miserable self.

NEVER worry about the misery of others.

NEVER worry about your debts, let your administrators do it.

NEVER worry about the comments and criticisms of your neighbors.

NEVER put yourself to any inconvenience to accomodate others.

NEVER subscribe to any local or other charities.

NEVER drink at your own expense.

NEVER give up your seat to women in a street car.

SPONGE all your reading.

BORROW all you can; lend nothing.

TAKE the biggest half of everything and the best seat in the house.

KICK on everything that is done for your comfort and make others as miserable as possible.

KNOCK everybody and point to yourself as the real "IT" and long life will be yours.

Occasionally a great temperance movement makes its appearance hereabouts. The goody, goody people raise their annual cry against the demon Rum. This only goes to show that "they know not whereof they speech." Truly for mildness and lack of intoxicating elements Horseheads' whiskey would put your communion wine to shame.

The scarcity of money to meet the demands of perpetual subscription lists, compels us to open a counterfeiting plant. Anyone having an outfit to dispose of or rent for a given period on a percentage basis, will kindly communicate with us by personal letter.

This is truly a great age—to think that even the old (would be) mother hen is robbed of her cherished hope of hatching a little Spring brood, by modern invention. If she has a will of her own and attempts to exert it, they tie a common red rag to her tail and kick her off the nest while the incubator usurps her right of kinship and robs her of that proud title "Mother." By golly, if I was an old hen and they treated me that way, I'd quit laying—blame me if I wouldn't.

The Winchester Optical Works is another institution that brings in outside money and distributes it among our tradesmen and employees. This establishment under the management of Mr. John Perkins, turns out spectacles by the million. John can fit you to a pair of glasses in two flits of a lamb's tail that will make your salary check look twice as large and will tell you in advance the extent of your crops before the sprouts are visible above ground. He also carries in stock an assortment of goggles in green, black and blue tints for those wishing to go into the alms business.

For Sale on Easy Terms.

A wooden leg seven years of age, sound except one knot-hole 1-2 inch in diameter nearly healed up with putty. Its owner wishing to give up a lucrative business to invest capital in real estate. Also a pair of green goggles and a sign to match with the words "Please Help the Blind." Address P. O. box No. 234. This guarantee goes with the outfit: The wooden leg was turned out of a sawlog discovered in Tuttle's millpond, the green goggles bear the imprint of the Winchester Optical Works and the sign was painted by a strolling sign painter who left with two weeks board and other marks of identification.

Our Post Master.

Give the town a boost by purchasing postage stamps and other government matter of T. J. Wintermute, our duly ordained postmaster.

"Jud" is a Republican by choice and bald-headed by nature. In spite of his years he handles the destinies of said office and its postage stamps with remarkable agility. He is ever courteous and does not hesitate to lick and append stamps to mail matter when requested to do so.

Our Undertakers.

It seems like sacrilige to joke about the undertaker, besides he has the final laugh , so it is well to tread lightly on sacred ground. Frank and George VanBuskirk are the two jolly undertakers of our town. I have placed Frank in the foreground because he is saving and stays at home nights, but George is an inveterate spendthrift. I have known him to start out on a cash job and when he reached home had not a sou Marquois to show for his days work. It is an undertaker's solemn duty to wear a manufactured smile so as to lighten if possible the distress of mourners. This George can do to perfection. Frank of course looks after the change that George brings back. In consequence he is more sedate and sad-eyed than his brother George. At any rate they are good fellows and attend promptly to calls and no complaint has ever been entered by those whom they have served.

It was so dry after the last temperance wave that farmers were obliged to bore holes in the soil with augers to sow their seeds and bait worms were bringing two shillings a dozen. ''That was some dry.''

Hon. R. P. Bush taking his political grist to the Albany mill.

❧ ❧ ❧ ❧ ❧

Jess Peck, Owner of Peck's Clean Coal Yard.
Coal delivered by wagon, auto, aeroplane and gasoline launch. Orders booked daily from El-

mira to Geneva. The only coal yard having a system of delivery by land or sea.

Our coal is put through a fresh water treatment by a natural process. When the creek is up and overflowing it finds its way into the coal bunkers, thus we have Clean Coal to offer to our trade. Jess Peck, proprietor, autoist and commodore of a fleet of one boat—the Ronomore.

Am pullets what's raised in a broodah as succulent as dem what's raised on dey muddah's breast? Ask Philo of Elmira, N. Y.

Our 4th of Julies.

At least once a year we advertise a Fourth of July celebration and say, when you see one of these functions advertised you want to put on your good clothes and come. It's nothing short of a 4-ring circus from start to finish. Only a few years ago a gorgeous display of pyrotecnics was billed as the grand finale to a joyous day. It was all of that and more too. Eighteen cold dollars were invested by the committee in pyro set pieces calculated to remind us of the father of his country and his favor to us by making us a free and equal people, but for lack of committee, fire drills and other preliminary preparations the whole bunch went off simultaneously (or I should say at once). I, being general manager of affairs and having the display under my supervision, left the neighborhood early for a point of safety where I might watch the grandeur of this closing feature. I did watch and what I saw baffles description. A thousand citizens with friends, bands and speakers had gathered to do honor and get all they could for nothing. A moment later the public square resembled a Bunker Hill battle field minus corpses. In their places there remained unclaimed sets of false teeth, hoop skirts, rubber shoes, parasols, and a raft of made over bonnets. The last seen of the band was its coat tails, each member headed for a special destination and still playing his part of the glorious Star Spangled Banner.

Aurelia Whitenack, Our Notary Public.

A man realizes his insignificance when he stands in the presence of a poor, weak woman clothed with government authority. Just fancy such a picture (if you can) of a three hundred pound "mutt" with his right palm in the air by command of a wee, tiny, sixty-pound maiden, swearing like a trooper to the authenticity of the contents of this book. Wouldn't it cause you to stretch the truth a bit? Maybe not. So you can bet everything these covers contain is as true as scripture and bears the seal of the state and the autograph of A. Whitenack, notary, B'Gosh.

Ex-Mayor Frank S. Bentley, Able Lawyer and Composer.

Author of that charming ballad "Forty Nine Blue Bottles were Hanging on the Wall." This

"NOW, ALL TOGEATHER!"

FORTY SEVEN BLUE BOTTLES A HANGING ON THE WALL, ETC.

delightful melody embraces an equal number of verses of the most delicious discord and other variations, each and every stanza having a striking resemblance to its next door neighbor.

Strange indeed that behind this man's stern, business-like exterior there lies hidden such a touch of tender poetic nature. If some of us had been born inside outward the world would be made the better for it no doubt, for that is the only way that hidden genius can be brought to the surface directly and successfully.

Our Foundries.

Horseheads has two large founderies, the Weller and Chas. Reeves, both plants running at full time the year round. Mr. Horace Weller is a sad looking man with a robust and happy family, so there is no excuse for his acting that way. I am at a loss to describe Mr. Reeves as he hides his countenance constantly behind a set of wicked looking whiskers, although I am told by those who once saw him emerge from his hiding, that he looks the part of a mild and generous soul, one who loves the Lord and could play a horn in the band, in consequence of which he was given an opportunity to blow himself by becoming a member. These two plants turn out everything in the way of castings and machine work, both are on the car line, so when you are out shopping for things made of pig iron you might stop in and examine their stock. The cars will wait for you while you make your purchases.

Our Blacksmiths.

Few towns can boast of four blacksmith shops within a radius of four blocks. Henry Nichols, Harry Burris, Al Card and Ed Van Gorden—

fearless fire-eaters and battle-scarred veterans of many encounters with kicking mules, etc—all trustworthy members of the craft, full of ginger and alive to the times. The blacksmith, like the poet, is not without honor.

What's your hurry? That's what I hear on all sides. Well I'll tell you all about it. I'm hurrying to Albany before the legislature adjourns to have Doc put through some amendments to our game laws. I got soaked once for carrying a ferret and I promise you now it shall never occur again.—NEVER AGAIN!

'If a hunter meet a hunter
Coming thro' the woods,
And each possess a little flask
Which contains the goods,
Should a body cry,
While pulling at the Rye?''
'Well I don't think.''

Special Notice!

This work is put out largely in the interest of the band for its equipment and maintenance. We must not overlook the fact that the erection of our band stand (which has so enthused the public and added to our last year's revenue) was built through the energy of A. P. Beard who collected the funds and donated his time and talent in its building. We intend to give the Horseheads public, its friends and neighbors a grand time this summer whenever the weather permits and on every occasion this book will be for sale to defray the expenses of the evening, for it costs money to run a band and keep up the enthusiasm of the musicians.

"Fitz."

As this goes to press an excavation is in progress in the atmosphere at the corner of John and Church streets where we are soon to behold a magnificent structure to be known as Fitz's Garage, where Fitz Crane, its proprietor, will be at your service to attend to the ills of your machine.

Orders will be booked for joy rides, etc.

Mr. Crane is past the voting age and stands sixteen hands high, and can take care of himself if necessary. We heartily recommend him to those wishing to pull off a vendue with good results. He also has a fine rabbit hound (free from fleas) which he will let out for the summer for his keeping. It will pay you to call on this versitile gentleman at his future garage, at the aforesaid address.

Things Will Disappear Even in the Presence of the Lord.

If the little green and innocent-looking step ladder that eloped with an unknown person from in front of our own door-step, will return to us, no questions will be asked and all will be forgiven.

The ladder came into our family when a wee infant, consequently its sudden disappearance is a great shock to my wife. She has become so accustomed to falling off this particular ladder while doing her semi-weekly house cleaning, that the poor distracted woman refuses to be consoled and declares she will never, no never, attempt to break in a new step-ladder, so I beg of you to allow yourself to be returned to us.

Mr. Tuttle's Mill.

If boards and planks could talk they might tell some harrowing tales of the harsh process of ripping and dressing which they endured while in the hands of Mr. Tuttle and his able lumbermen. This sawmill is one of the best equipped and most complete in the country. So modern is this plant that not a single by-product is wasted. The sawdust is made into breakfast food. Hard knots are ground up into Skotch snuff and the pitch extracted by a kiln process is converted into chewing gum and used by the employees to break them of the tobacco habit.

"NEXT VICTIM!"

Barbers.

They say that the safety razor has discouragingly eaten into the barber's profits. Please tell me then how Joe Steiger can build a fine brick house with modern heating system, and how Bill Wightman can purchase a filly with an enviable record, and five bushels of chopped feed, at the same time, if there is no money in training whiskers.

DOES THE RAZOR HURT?

While the historian had no intention to touch upon church matters but simply industrial affairs he cannot overlook the progressiveness of our mutual friend the Rev. Father Winters. Recently the good Father exhibited a subscription list which I afterwards found to be for the benefit of St. Joseph's hospital. The flaunting of such a document is akin to shaking the crimson rag in a bull's face and acts as an immediate challange to a marathon. I accepted the challenge of course, and straightway proceeded down the Avenue having the good Father handicapped by two blocks, but soon my steampipes gave out and I was forced to cough up $10 and glad was I that this accident befel me, for I felt much better to know that my coughing spell was for so good a cause.

Seriously speaking, this is only one sample of the Noble Causes that always enlist the unselfish

sympathies of Father Winters. Since his coming amongst us he has proved himself to be a most devoted, dignified and consistent Churchman as well as a most public-spirited and broad-minded Citizen. Verily both Church and State can be proud of men of Father Winters' Character and Ability.

The Chink.

Twice to our best recollection we have been threatened with the yellow peril. You Sing and He Sing, both laundrymen (which is a remarkable co-incidence) were located on the Bowery, and showed their oriental good taste by keeping to themselves. Our foreign element is quite limited. We have a few Ginnies, three Hebrews and two Swiss Warblers, otherwise we are strictly Americans.

Final tribute to poor ''Patsy'' to whom this volume is so pathetically dedicated. He had many friends, likewise many enemies. The memory of his friends he carried with him to the grave and perhaps to dog heaven. His enemies he banished from his mind and body without mercy ere he passed into eternity.

Our Livery and Exchange Stables.

We are well equipped with livery stables—having two—where a fine collection of spavins and ringbones are ever at your service. The price of livery hire is moderate and if you are shy the cash we will carry your account for an indefinite period. If you have the time to spare kindly stop

and look over our swapping stock which we guarantee sound as a sponge and in every way worthy of a change in life.

Whenever one refers to the name Eisenhart the answer comes "which one, Ollie or the old man?" It is evident that there are but two Eisenharts, R. G. and O. D. This treats with the elder, (so-called old man,) but make no mistake, he is not the sort of man who looks into decline. Every year he adds another foot of solid brick and mortar to his chimney which is already 125 feet tall. You must

"DER SCHMOKE COMDT YETZ FON DEM CHIMNEY OUS."

not measure the man's longevity with the altitude of his smoke stack however.

In the upbuild of Horseheads Mr. Eisenhart has taken an important part. For many years he was president of the village, and discharged the duties of that office to the perfect satisfaction of all. He is a strict churchman. Probably that is the only charge against him. Mr. Eisenhart believes in the future of the soul, also the future price of pressed brick, as he is holding several million of the latter for an advance in the market price.

His motto is "never look backwards." Keep your eyes straight ahead at the $ sign. If this were not so wouldn't he take up his pen and say some things to some folks? Oh, no! I guess not! My apologies and good will. I intended no harm in the foregoing remarks.

Mr. Eisenhart Sr., is such a busy man that the artist had some difficulty in getting a true picture of him. It might be well to add the following description to aid the imagination, viz: Disguised as a laborer, no diamonds, Ingersoll watch with shoe string guard, bald ring beneath the rear of his tile and brick dust on his boots.

The Sayre Shoe Factory.

Away down in the south west corner of our beautiful village, hidden beneath a cluster of maples, where a little stream of smoke is seen wending its way heavenward, nestles the Geo. M. Sayre Kiddy Shoe Factory. Like the workshop of a Santa Claus, wherein forty (more or less) fairies busy themselves in the making of little shoes for the infant world. One can judge of the tremendous growth of this great Republic by looking over George's order books from year to year, and one will also arrive at one conclusion that race suicide is quite unpopular in our land of the free and home of the brave.

When we speak of Williams the MAP MAN we mean Prof. F. D. Williams who has perhaps the most unique shop in town. He makes outline

NO NEED OF BEING A DUNCE IF YOU STUDY MY MAPS.

maps for school purposes. Strangers suffering with tanglefoot and addicted to staying out late nights will find them a great convenience in determining short cuts and bee lines across country.

Regarding the Fertility of Our Soil.

One needs only to pass along the highway or the trolley line toward Watkins to find a vision in modern gardening—a veritable wonderland. Looking across the celery gardens of James Cromwell, Russ Treat, Ed Treat and the Donovan Brothers from an elevation of perhaps fifty feet, (the highway) this expanse of muck bears a perfect likeness to a choice piece of dress goods of your wife's selection, the rows of celery and onion sprouts with an acre boquet of lettuce here and there to break the beautiful monotany of exactness reminds one of his unpaid milliner and dress-maker bills. For that reason alone we advise a trip of inspection, even if it proves of no interest to you personally prayers may be offered up for us for having called your attention to the aforesaid unpaid bills. We take it from those who know that the only comparison is heaven but if you are not yet ready to go to such extremes we recommend a trip by auto or trolley or one of John Colwell's wind-broken spavins.

Hello! Here is our old friend and former resident, George H. Beard, who travels for Clawson & Wilson Co. of Buffalo, N. Y. George helped lay the corner stone of prosperity then he dug out for a colder clime, Auburn, N. Y. George carries a fine line of habberdasher goods—overalls and pants, hats, caps, mittens and underwear. He always finds a glad hand awaiting him either to work him for the drinks or visa-versa.

Charles A. Brown, druggist and commodore of the yacht Yankee Doodle, holds the record for the largest German brown trout ever caught in this locality. The prize trout weighed over seven pounds and measured 27 inches in his stocking feet. The commodore always backs up his fish tales by putting the goods in evidence, and to settle the matter for all time to come he has it mounted and hung in his laboratory where skeptics may look and measure and feel and pinch to their hearts' content.

Being a close friend he was kind enough to let the author into the secret of catching big ones but

cautioned him to treat the matter confidentially. I take said he, a large hook and spit on it, then I put on about half pound of calves liver, cast in, then I set and wait. You see when the trout hear the noon whistles tooting they know it's time for dinner. Naturally the big trout get home before the little ones so when they discover that some neighbor has brought in a delicacy it sharpens up their appetites and they are right well pleased.

After landing one of these trout the creek bank looks like a prize ring where a 24 round mill has been pulled off and the angler has much use for arnica and court plaster.

One should not pass through Horseheads without visiting Archie Turner's Ostridge-Shetland farm. Bus runs every half hour from the Platt House, giving the sightseer ample time to look over his stock, listen to good stories and catch his train the next morning.

The author wishes to extend his thanks to Gen. Sullivan, "Big Chief Red Jacket" and all those concerned in making early history for without their co-operation this book would have been unheard of and the capital of our numerous advertisers would have remained uninvested and an appreciative reading public wrongfully robbed of a "good thing."

The recent demise of my old friend Enos Cook compels me to omit much that would interest the reader. Enos was a good old soul chuck full of fish stories and lovable manly traits, honest to the core and in fact the most interesting character of his time. Among lovers of rod and gun his memory will never tarnish.

The Horseheads High School is one of the best
educational institutions in the state. It takes the
child in the rough, as it were, and turns it out in
polished academic order ready for college or pre-
pared to fill a position as teacher of a district
school.

Parents in other parts wishing to rear their
children in a creditable and satisfactory manner
should break camp at once and move to Horseheads. We do not wallop education into the
tender child but teach it by a system of kindness
and patience to become proficient and self-sup-
porting. Some years ago a professor tried to wallop knowledge into a boy without first inquiring
into the lad's pugilistic powers—thus another
professor had to be appointed to fill his place

while a surgeon picked out the slivers from his
anatomy.

Thank heaven we have now a kind-hearted, in-
telligent man as principal and a corps of able
teachers, also a janitor of much experience who
looks after the comforts of the little ones, regu-

lates the atmosphere and destroys the microbes liable to linger about a school room.

To the taxpayers is due the credit for the selection of the high brow, able and well seasoned board of education with which we are blessed.

How well I remember the day I was up before the board—facing an audience of mothers and fathers—wrestling with a recitation that ran something like this: "My name is Norval and on the Grampion hills my father feeds his flock,etc." while over in another corner of the great recitation chamber sat a rival of mine pelting spit balls at me through a putty blower.

This history would not be complete without some mention of one of our old timers who flip-flopped into fame some time in the sixties. Horseheads has turned out many able statesmen but how many celebrated clowns has she given to the world? Only one. Charles Seeley is the man who holds that distinction, his flip-flops were executed with such ease and grace that they became as popular and as much sought for as our grandmothers' pancakes. It was a long jump from the tan bark on the banks of the old canal to the circus ring of the biggest show on earth. That's what happened to Charlie and he is now located at No. 1 Easy street.

**To the Officials of the Railroad that Carried Me
Safely to My Destination:**

I hope I am not libelling the D. L. & W. R. R.
Co. if I make the following statement (under oath)
that I have traveled over your system nigh onto
twenty years and I have never encountered a
wreck or discourtesy in all the thousands of miles
I have covered. When I enter your coaches I feel
as secure as though I were tucked away in a safe
deposit vault, and far more comfortable. I will
relate an actual incident which may cause Phebe
Snow to turn green with envy. It happened one
dark and gloomy night, the air was drizzling with
drizzle, my chickens were down with the pips,
spring garden stuff was dragging along in a most

miserable way and I was heart-sick over affairs in
general. Time came for me to embark for the

great city of New York—to toil and reap the re-
ward for which my creditors at home were wait-
ing—my aspect was that of abject misery, my
celluloid collar and cuffs were soiled and my clothing damp and shapeless. I felt like a deserted
morgue when I climbed into my berth. I cared
not a fiddlestick whether school kept or not. I
slept when I was not awake, and presently I slept
some more, finally morning arrived, so did the
train without serious mishap to either. The
porter nudged me and yelled Hoboken. I found
my shirt, collar and cuffs immaculately white, my
shoes were burnished, my clothing pressed and
spots removed, the morguelike feeling had also
vanished and I was happy and hungry as a horse.
For a moment I was bewildered, then I remembered where I was at,for the jolly porter was hum-
ming this sweet refrain:

"If travel you must on a drizzly night
    Better stick to the road of Anthracite."
P. S.   His palm was out to bid me god speed so
I dropped in a five spot and urged him to buy some
trinkets for his wives along the lovely road of
Anthracite.

Police Justice's Special Notice.

We quote here a table of cut rates for the benefit of those who have transgressed and who for
personal reasons have no desire to patronize their
home justice of the peace:

First offense, to strangers $5.00
Second offense, six months with board and lodging
    P. S.—Guests must come well recommended.

A question we'd like to have answered:
    Can a sick hen lay a well egg?

THE SILENT CITY ON GRASSHOPPER HILL.

Every respectable community should possess a cemetery. It is a public necessity and a good business proposition, in fact it is about the only real estate that is always self-sustaining regardless of the financial condition of the country. Cemetery stock never fluctuates. It is not hampered by business rivalry nor is it at the mercy of greedy trusts. It is a safe and sane investment. The community should see also that the property is kept in a cheerful and inviting state and garbed with an air of welcome.

Horseheads may well feel proud of its beautiful silent city where all is peace and harmony, where not one of its hundreds of occupants was ever heard to utter an unkind word against his next door neighbor and where the solemn, ancient tombstone gives its reasons for being erected, in such rare poetic pathos as this:

> Beneath this mound
> Lies Uncle Jim
> His seventh wife was—
> Too much for him.

> So stranger as you wander by
> Let not this tomb escape your eye;
> His seventh time of married bliss
> Fetched Jim, the poor old soul, to this.

Note—Yes indeed. When it comes to tucking you away for keeps we can assure you as good a time as anyone else owning a cemetery and you won't regret it either.

Behold our mutual friend Chas. O. Tuttle of jig-saw fame. Charlie will be remembered by the patrons of our successful fairs as the man who did all the jig-saw work. He is without a doubt the handiest man at rapid filigree work in the world. He was appointed first lieutenant to the designer and promoter of Masonic and Firemen fairs, which office he holds until death-duth-uth-part.

Mr. C. O. Tuttle is a brother to W. E. Tuttle, the two original (senior) Tuttle Bros. A branch owned and operated by the (junior) Tuttle Bros., is located at Westfield, N. J. Congressman "Will" Tuttle helps to run the machinery of the government whilst his youthful brother "Art" keeps his eye on the machinery of the lumber mill and coal yard. We regret to say that unless the latter two change their condition matrimonially the name Tuttle will eventually perish on the sands of time. Better get busy boys!

"MORT" BENTLEY.

Who takes care of the fish producing end of the Bentley & Bills market. When the lake trout get a sight of Mort they just keel over and come to the top.

FRANK BILLS

Whose succulent soup bones have a world wide reputation.

JOHN DAILEY
Who speaks only the truth and sticks to it.

JEROME R. PLATT.
A young and enthusiastic member of the Cashmere Grotto of Elmira, cold water advocate (for washing purposes) and a citizen of esteem.

ROY L. BOWERS.

Noble Knight of the Greasy Monkey Wrench.
Official turnkey of the village water system. The
man who mends our leaks and at the same time

makes more. Every community must have such
a person. Roy is ours.

Open Season on Cod Fish Balls

The open season for spearing cod-fish balls is
from Jan. 1 to Dec. 31 (in all states). They may
be taken by fair or foul means, any time when not
nesting (in hot fat). The C. F. B. inhabits the
narrow confines of certain cafes and are of many
varieties. Anyone caught spearing more than
three balls without taking out a fresh license at
the bar for each offence shall be deemed a viola-
tor and subject to mutilation and eviction by the
proprietors of said cafes. There shall be no limit
to size of the pursued,any size that are easily slipped down the throat without mastication will come
within this law.

Cheerful Billy Phillips, our trustworthy operator at the Northern Central Station.

His business consists of directing the unseen juice over the wire for the Postal Telegraph Co., and keeping the engineers busy reaching for orders, so that trains going in opposite directions on a single track will hesitate before proceeding.

CHANDLER A. HAMMOND.

There is hardly a man in the world but has some mark of distinction. Mr. Hammond's rare individuality lies in his feet. He is proud of the fact that he carries the largest line of shoe leather upon his person of any man in town. It is safe to remark that the grass never grows beneath his feet. Chandy is a good Elk and a thousand and one other kinds of good things which this picture endeavors to portray. Any man who can stand such abuse is truly my friend and a good fellow.

"Doc" Dean vs. "Jim" Dean, Local Champions.
"Sam" spends most of his time jerking molars (without pain) when not engaged in the manly art of checkers, and Jim would miss a calf deal any time to get in mortal combat with his adversary.

It ought to be a source of consolation to the poor man to know that even if he cannot revel in all the luxuries of the rich he can at least be his equal in the ownership of corns and bunion., for the Lord decreed that they should be equally dis tributed among rich and poor alike.

Edward A. VanGorden, Blacksmith

At whose blacksmith studio the latest news is dispensed from 7 a. m. to 6 p. m. Unlike the barber, he only listens and when gossip reaches the white heat stage he pounds his anvil most vigorously to temper down the minds of his flock. Ed is a splendid type of good Shepherd, though he has many crooks on his staff. When it comes to blacksmithing Ed can forge anything but a check. His dominating trait is minding his own business, his only bad one is smoking two cigars a day. Really too good for a minister his father brought him up a blacksmith, a fine example of the 50th period covered abundantly with local glory and axle grease.

For Shame.

And to think that you should allow your heels to run over and expose your sole so shamefully when we are blessed with two of the world's finest cobblers—August Braun and James Donahue.

Don't try to gulp down more than your skin will hold. It is very bad form and a grave injustice to your system to persist in forcing down "just one more," when you find your hoops have already reached their limit of expansion. Be moderate in manipulating the wet goods I beseech thee.

HON. L. M. BROWN

Lord of the High Court of Justice of Horseheads.
Whose wise and unbiased judgment of men and their deeds has landed many (worthy of such fate) across the threshhold of the bastile.

Some men were born with a silver spoon in their mouth. In proportion to the size of some mouths a soup ladle would have been more appropriate.

Tuneful lines applicable to July 4th, 1911, 800
feet above sea level and a radius of 400,000 degrees
forninst Hanover Square, Horseheads, N. Y.
"I love my light weight summer suit,
But Oh! you Adam and Leaves."

Those who deserve honorable mention but won't
get it.

REGARDING OUR M. D.'s.

It is hardly worth while ailing in Horseheads. We used to welcome the mumps, measles or chicken-pox as a relief from business worry. But, bless —your—soul, we are surrounded by such a for-

midable battery of physicians and surgeons that before one has time to realize the pleasures of disease they have him on his pins again struggling for existence. No sir; if you have to grunt and ail Horseheads is no place for you.

Telephonic conversation between her highness the cook and the roundsman on her beat.

"Hello! Officer Doogan!" "Hello Doo-gy," is that yez? Say how'd yez like to make yer rounds of the beat in me motor car tonight? Yes this is Katie the cook at Goulderbilt's. Alright, I'll have the missus and her daughter the Dootchess of Rasberry wash me dinner dishes and I'll call for yez at seven—but mind yez! Not a word of this to yer woife."

Peck's Grist Mill.

Where itch is extracted from Home Spun Buck-
wheat by a modern process and without pain.
George Peck, its proprietor, claims to own the

secret of extracting the itch direct from the original kernal. We are, therefore, indebted to Mr.
Peck for the absence upon our human surface of
the many pimples of former years.

THE POPULAR SUMMER GAME — SWATTING
FLIES FOR THE LEMONADE (?)

Let us confine ourselves to the fly. Do you realize that the greatest trust of all is the fly trust, we
place implicit confidence in him, tender him the
freedom of our house and go away for the summer while this measly, pesky ingrate proceeds to

make love to numberless other flies, gets married
and goes on multiplying by the millions.
Then comes the pilfering of your sugar and other
things suiting his taste. Did you ever stop to
figure out what a million grains of sugar means

on your grocery bill? You'd "fire" your hired
girl for it, you'd send an ordinary burglar to states
prison and you'd politely request your grocery-
man to tear your page out of his ledger and warn
him never to show his face in your vicinity again.
That's what you'd do and nothing less.

Some years ago the history of Chemung county
was written by Ausburn Towner as you will remember. It is a great book of records, a general
information bureau. I own a copy and heartily
recommend it to lovers of historical truth, also
to those who wish to pry into the age of some old
maid neighbors or the number of times some much
envied grass widow has entered into the holy
bonds of matrimony. It is a book as authentic
as "Hoyle" in settling disputes of that sort. In
my history, however, I give you the bare, unadult-
erated facts concerning the menfolks. I know
enough to let alone the weaker sex, or at least to

speak of them with reverence and without question regarding their ages whenever that subject is introduced, for a woman single handed ill-disposed toward me has the power in her tongue (heaven bless her) to smash my ambitions of a quarter of a century and bring to earth all that I have accomplished. "Oh woman heaven bless thee, for without thee where would we be at?"

FRED. BENTLEY. BACK ON THE FARM.

**Our Friend Fred Bentley
Among His Native Highballs.**

Lazy Day Sporting Events

Pitching pennies to the crack has been cut out of the list of events for the season at least, the authorities having decided it gambling.

The Horseheads Construction Co. is ready to furnish figures on concrete work of any nature. They are just closing a contract to build a concrete bridge across the Atlantic. The work will be under the supervision of an able engineer by the name of Ezra Walker. There has been much talk about the town regarding this contemplated bridge but the bridge is bound to come, so Ezra says, and when it is built you bet we'll have it connect with Newtown Creek so that our wares will be in the London market every morning before breakfast.

THE 'EVER GLORIOUS' WAS A DRY ONE FOR SURE.' WATER WORKS ON THE BUMM ETC.

LAUREN THOMAS
Who makes more noise to the inch than any member of the band.

Notable epochs before the closing of the nineteenth century:

When the Chemung Canal evaporated.

When the village was mortgaged to the E. C. & N. R. R. Co.

And when Ene Cook shot the cast iron frog.

RUFUS
Once a Handsome Child.

"SAM" THE NOZZLEMAN.

"MORE PRESSURE
MR FIREMAN, OR
YOU'LL NEVER
QUENCH OUR THIRST."

SAM RANDOLPH
An Active and Enthusiastic Fireman.

"BENNY"
The Landscape Artist.

Manufacturers who contemplate a change of residence will do well to look over our desirable land which we are holding for that purpose. We are fenced in by trunk line railroads. A shipping center that "can't be beat." Here your employees may find all sorts of recreation, cheap living, good houses with gardens, low rents, excellent society, churches of all denominations and a good safe bank to lay aside a fortune for a rainy day.

One foot in the air and the other upon a banana peel places a man in a most uncertain position.

A Letter From a Fond Mother.

Mr. E. Zim:

Dear Sir: I noticed in a magazine article on your early life, that you once worked for a fish peddler. I have a red-headed boy of 12 who exhibits marked signs of future greatness—mostly in the line of comic art. Will you please recommend a competent fish peddler who would be willing to start my boy on his art career and thus confer an everlasting favor upon an anxious mother? Very sincerely,

Mrs. So-ond-So.

Mrs. So-and-So:

Dear Madam: It pains me to state that there are no more fish peddlers, the profession having died with Bill Marshall (my boss). Fish are now ordered by phone and delivered in automobiles; besides there are no longer such fish as Bill Marshall peddled. They died long before Bill and his profession and long before they were allowed to grace a plank. We have a board of health now who regulate the sale of fish. Unless your son can procure a permit from the said board of health to push a fish cart for a year or two he might as well banish the idea of becoming a comic artist. Regretfully yours,

ZIM.

Some people are continually entreating their Creator to remove them from this world of sin unto His kingdom of eternal joy and rest, yet the minute they have the slightest bellyache they rush for a doctor who proceeds forthwith to end that much coveted journey.

Don't allow the spirit of jealousy to take possession of your better self just because your neighbor affords a half dozen automobiles and you have none. I remember when fleas were a luxury if one did not possess an overabundance, but fleas like autos become an annoyance when one owns too many.

Blessed be he who reacheth down from his lofty perch and lendeth the lowly beggar a helping hand.

HIS EXCELLENCY "LORD MAYOR" HATHAWAY.

COLLINS L. HATHAWAY

A complete eulogy of this potentate may be found on pages 16-17.

That Peskiest of Pests.

Why do I entertain a special antipathy for the house fly? It is not because the imp bathed in my soup, nor is it that he skates upon my bald head, for I own no bald head, but for an inexcusable joke played on me while I was endeavoring to select a restful and isolated spot where I might enjoy a week of needed vacation. It happened this way: I was at the depot perusing the rail road map in search of a place sufficiently removed from work and worry and out of the public gaze. It was then that this infernal pest did his dark deed. Watching me like a land shark and as mine eyes closed for a moment in dreams of vacation bliss, he crept to an obscure point of the line and placed thereat a mark suggestive of a small isolated station. I selected that very spot as the destination for my outing, purchased a ticket and requested the engineer (as a special favor) to slow down his train and drop me off at this nameless point. When I alighted I found naught but swamps and mosquitoes. Chagrined to the core I walked twenty hot and dusty miles to the nearest station and returned home to demand that my fare be refunded. The ticket agent demurred. A careful microscopic analysis of the map reveal-the fact that said spot was not of printers' ink nor the work of human hands. My suspicion immediately fell upon the fly, now I'm after his b-l-o-o-d—cur-s-s-se him.

The man who trusts to the honesty of his fellowman comes out ahead every time.

The man looking for trouble usually finds it even if he has to manufacture it himself.

The man who continually suspects the world of cheating him out of his rights is really cheating himself.

"OH – HI – TEE – DEE – TIE – DIE; HI – TEE – DEE,
GET – YER – GAL, AND – WALTZ – ALONG – WITH – ME."

PROF. FRED AHART.

This gentleman is open for engagements at **all** seasons of the year; makes a specialty of midnight calls. Anyone troubled with insomnia and feeling the need of a breakdown or an Irish reel before retiring can get it by depositing three kicks into the lower panels of his front door and making their wishes known.

Again I must ask you to excuse (what may seem bad spelling) or typo errors. In Horseheads **we** have a system of our own, a knack of spelling by ear. We will take for instance the word "Sassy phras" or "musher-rooms" or "cupillo." It certainly sounds more musical in our native tongue (or "tung") than in the prosaic, simon pure Webster dictionary intonation and decidedly original.

Ode to My Old Setting Hen

Written for a Snare Drum Accompaniment.

An agent, one of the slickest of men,
  With brooders and hatchers galore,
Rapped at the coop of my old setting hen
  And proceeded to open the door.
      (2nd verse worse than the 1st verse.)
I came to palm off a brooder said he
  It will lighten your labors, I beg to infer,
I bid thee skidoo Mr. Agent said she
  The old-fashioned method I really prefer.

I look upon the late General Sullivan (I am proud to state) as a close personal friend and benefactor, as it was through his valor that I met my wife in Horseheads, for had he christened the place Bullheads instead I should most certainly have been obliged to meet those who now call me husband and father at Bullheads of course. I am so ashamed of some of this repartee that I am almost tempted to hand back your currency, but that would be undignified and very, very unprofessional. Allow me to remark that if you purchased this book with good money and without a murmur of protest then there is truth after all in the statement of the late P. T. Barnum that the public likes to be humbugged.

Sporting News.

Wife—Where did you read the account of Bliv-in's suicide.

Husband—On the sporting page my dear; third column.

Some faces which (through no fault of ours) escaped the rogues' gallery.

I trust a copy of this book will reach the notice of the following persons for the following reasons:

Androo Carnage-e in the hope that he will take a general interest in the village of Horseheads and a special personal interest in the author of this work.

John D. Stonefeller that he may be inspired to offer up special prayers for the success of the book.

J. Bierponch Morguen that he may be tempted to purchase (at a flattering price) the original manuscript and drawings and bury the same in some mouldy museum out of the sight and reach of the author.

Hetty Green in hope that she may assume the sole agency for the U. S. and advance some change to enlarge our facilities and hire another union printer to relieve our overworked staff and otherwise congested conditions.

Bill Tafft trusting that he will mention the book in his next important message to congress.

A most despicable man is he who is afraid to express an opinion—and a gol-darn Jackass if he does.

Exasperating.

Wife (angrily)—I ought never to have married you!

Husband (sarcastically)—Hum! You'd look nice trying to button up your dress in the back without me!

A Voice of Caution to the Farmer.

Every locality has its theoratical farmers. We have about twice as many to the acreage as any locality. These men of agricultural brain matter sit in a morris chair all day and direct the destinies of their neghbors' farms. They can cultivate more land and raise more stuff (on paper) than the Lord ever calculated that land to produce. A man who wilfully robs the soil with figures is downright mean and I aint ashamed to say so neither.

SAYRE, WATCHING THE MONEY END OF THE COW.

J. Sayre Holbert

The Laceyville Manager of the Horseheads Creamery Co.

A traveling salesman who was detained by floods when informed of his mother-in-law's death wired home: "Go ahead with festivities; wash out; can't come."

Three Faithful Servants of the Public at Large

We have among us many who deserve honorable mention, but for the respect in which they are held in the community, their dear old gray whiskers and for the sake of their loving wives and children who do not wish to see the handsome features of their kin so mercilessly mutilated we must omit them.

Sam Taber, the old "Horseheads Philosopher" who, in the course of the past 85 years, has tested everything drinkable, from cistern water to vitriol has this to say of the drink habit. He says says he, "that there is no harm in drinking but it's this drinking between drinks what raises the devil with a feller."

FRANK — & — GEORGE.
AT YOUR SERVICE.

The Jolly Undertakers,

Referred to in another part of the Book.

The "stuff" in this book was only intended to interest the people of Chemung county. If others have had the audacity to read it and it has afforded them any pleasure it serves them good and right and they need look for no sympathy from the author.

Since the world began, religion has passed through many changes. Not so with Satan, he conducts his business in his same old way and seems to be prosperous as ever.

Bogardus the Photographer
Who is largely responsible for the handsome visages in this book.

THE E., H. & W. TROLLEY.

A delightful ride is that which leads to Watkins Glen by the Elmira, Horseheads and Watkins trolley.

It winds you through seventeen miles of incomparable valley scenery—where you may behold the "Rube" in his natural state, (principally York state.) The kind hearted and accommodating conductors and motormen will look out for the comfort and safety of children while their mothers alight to pick wild flowers and berries along the line.

Dan Perkins

Our dutiful Village Clerk.

If you are a scrappy person and want excitement, come to Horseheads.

If you have a peaceable disposition and want comfort and ease, come to Horseheads.

We don't drink, but if you insist, come to Horseheads.

If you want to join us, come to Horseheads.

If you have a fat wad to invest, come to Horseheads.

On entering the town from either direction you
will find courteous guides at hand to show you to
all the places of interest.

The way to tell when you are entering the do-
main (dough-main) first (on leaving Elmira) take
a liberal drink, then get on the car and by the time
your thirst returns you are in Horseheads. Three
hotels are provided at this point for the purpose
of alleviating your condition.

Joe Burns of New York

Special Messenger sent by the Standard Oil Co. to
secure the first copy of this book for
the Rockefeller Library.

The Zim Band like its namesake, the Zim Cigar,
is getting along nicely and so are those who par-
take of them.

John Barlow is perhaps the most faithful servant of our fire brigade. John is a charter member and has worn the white helmet more than one season, besides he has occupied almost every office in the department. John has a different ailment for each month, yet he is never too ill to join a party of sarsaphras diggers, and forgets his aches and pains at the first tap of the fire bell.

This work (understand) has undergone the scrutiny of the town censor and an advisory board and is placed on the market subject to the pure food laws of nineteen-'leven. Consequently we must abide by said ruling and you dear purchaser and reader must tolerate these contents.

Regarding Jake Greatsinger, one of our pioneers, to whom the destinies of the locality were entrusted by General Sullivan himself. He is too shy and coy to permit of his picture being used in this work but I remember when he hadn't his pockets full of trolley lines and he was willing to stand for anything.

APPENDIX.

Dear Reader:

I call this part of my book the "Appendix," for the simple reason that the book (as a literary gem) would thrive as well, or better, without it, therefore, should it prove a source of annoyance to you I recommend that you avail yourself of its removal as speedily as possible. Before doing so, however, kindly read it over and make sure that you are unable to forbear the torture, and for this consideration my everlasting thanks.

The Author.

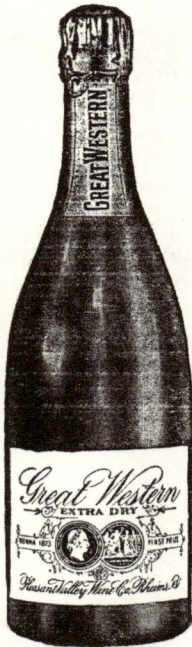

FREDERICK C. TOMLINSON

Specialist In

Casualty & Automobile Insurance

111 WEST WATER STREET

Elmira - - **New York**

If you've got any shifting around to do call for BELA TIFFT, the Horseheads Drayman. He's a Crackerjack.

Now ladies and gentlemen, brothers and sisters, aunts, uncles and cousins:

If you have a son or your neighbor has a son and his son has a son who has a son artistically inclined you should get for him

ZIM'S Book
"This and That" about Caricature
$1.50 BY MAIL

It treats entirely on

COMIC ART & CARICATURE

Tells him what to do and don't. Remit by check, postal or express money order.

E. ZIM.

Horseheads   New York.

"OCH DU LIEBER LOBSTER !"

The Oldest Place in the City.

BILLY HOFFMAN'S CAFE
E. Water St., Elmira.

J. L. CHURCHILL

MONUMENT DEALER
TWO COMPLETE FACTORIES.
IMMENSE STOCK ON HAND

Horseheads, N. Y.   Elmira, N. Y.

Work of Highest Quality delivered and set in any part of the United States without extra charge.

Address Mail 1102 Walnut St. Elmira, N. Y. Both Phones.

THE ZIM BAND UNIFORMED BY THE E. G. CROWELL CO OF ELMIRA, N. Y.

McCann's Tours

Personally Conducted
J. P. Mc CANN

■ ■ ■ ■ ■ ■

47 West 34th Street
NEW YORK CITY.

■ ■ ■ ■ ■ ■

WRITE FOR INFORMATION REGARDING
AMERICAN AND EUROPEAN TOURS

Subscribe for the Tourist Magazine.

J. P. MC CANN PUBLISHING CO.
NEW YORK

D. F. LANE President and Treasurer

GEO D. CASE Vice-Pres. and Sec'y.

The Lane Bridge Company

ENGINEERS AND CONTRACTORS

Designs

and

Estimates Furnished

Works and Office

PAINTED POST, N. Y.

Manufacturers of

STEEL BRIDGES

BUILDINGS

STRUCTURAL WORK

ARCHES

SLUICE PIPE

—AND—

BRIDGE FOUNDATIONS

OF ALL KINDS

Carry in Stock

ANGLES   BEAMS

CHANNELS   PLATES

RAILROAD RAILS

STEEL BARS, ETC.,

FOR IMMEDIATE USE

STRUCTURAL CAST IRON

FURNISHED ON SHORT

NOTICE

EXCHANGE MILLS

FLOUR AND FEED

PURE BUCKWHEAT FLOUR

A SPECIALTY

GEO. C. PECK

Proprietor

F

THE CHEMUNG VALLEY REPORTER

Prints Everything It Gets a Chance To.

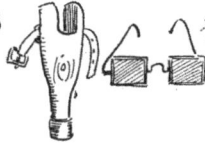

THERE'S HEAPS OF COMFORT IN PECK'S CLEAN COAL, AND NOT A PARTICLE OF SLATE.

LOOKS GOOD, TASTES GOOD & IS GOOD. "MAKES A PERFECT BLEND."

BILLY.

BREESPORT WATER.

Wᵐ J. LORMORE

The Celebrated Breesport Oxygenated Water.

WM. J. LORMER, ELMIRA, N. Y.

L. L. Laskaris
ICE CREAM MFGR.

Elmira, N. Y. - *Always Ready.*

We Clothe a Lot of Horseheads

But Have Never Had a
Look In From "ZIM."

REID & WINNER

104 W. WATER ST. - - ELMIRA, N. Y.

M A N D E R ' S
BREWING CO.

Finest in the Land—So Everybody Says.

The occupants of this Winton Car were raised on Horseheads Creamery Co.'s Pasteurized Milk.
Mr. and Mrs. O. D. Eisenhart and family.

A Gunning We'll Go

We are gunning for your trade in Guns, Ammunition, Fishing Tackle, Hunting Boots, Coats, Leggings, Gun Cases and everything in the Sporting and Outing Goods line.

OUR POLICY—We carry the standard makes in all lines. We're not looking for the "extra profit" on the "just-as-good" kind. Mail orders receive prompt attention.

ELMIRA ARMS CO.

Wholesale and Retail.   117 Main St., Elmira.

THE

STAR GAZETTE

The Only

Evening Paper

In The City Of Elmira.

ENTERPRISE CUT GLASS CO.,

Manufacturers of

FINE GLASSWARE

Elmira Heights,   -   -   -   New York

No. 1040 Whiskey Jug   Rambler Rose

This bottle is built on the square; would look particularly fine on your sideboard with something in it.

FAMOUS IRONWEAR HALF HOSE

SIX PAIR GUARANTEED TO WEAR 6 MONTHS

Guarantee their Product to be the Best Half Hose for the price in the world.

They Guarantee Six Pair to wear **SIX MONTHS** without darning. If they fail will give to the purchaser 6 new pair Free of Charge.

Blue, Brown, Helio, Gray, Wine, Black.

Look Like Silk
Feel Like Silk
Wear Like Iron

Chemung County Agricultural Society

Fifty Second Annual Exhibition

Sept. 18-19 20-21-22, 1911.

OPEN DAY AND NIGHT

"MEET US AT THE COUNTY FAIR," MAW-PAW AND THE BABY.

PLATT HOUSE

Horseheads, N. Y.

J. R. PLATT, Prop.

Automobile Headquarters

Barns and Sheds for Horses.

About ZIM...........

Eugene Zimmerman was born in Basel, Switzerland, on May 26, 1862. The death of his mother in 1864 split the family, and in 1867, he emigrated with his father and brother to New Jersey. His artistic career launched when he apprenticed himself to sign painter William Brassinger, who recently moved to Elmira, New York. Eugene earned little as a painter's apprentice but gained valuable experience. Eugene lived with his employer's family at 303 South Main Street.

In 1880, he took a job at a rival sign firm in nearby Horseheads, New York. In his spare time, he copied the work of other cartoonists. The nearby Syracuse *Telegram* newspaper recognized his potential. Eugene took the name "Zim" as his professional name. The few drawings that Zim published in the *Telegram* made their way to the politically humorous Puck magazine editors. *Puck* quickly hired Zim in 1883. He left *Puck* for *Judge* in 1885. Editors at *Judge* appreciated Zim's ability to satirize both urban and rural life. In 1886, Zim married Mable Alice Beard of Horseheads. For a brief time, they resided in Brooklyn, but because both preferred the quiet rural life, they came back to Horseheads. Every other week Zim commuted to New York for consultations with the *Judge* staff but did most of his drawing in Horseheads.

Zim was the founder of the "Grotesque" school of caricature and was the first caricaturist to incorporate exaggerated features not only in the faces of his subjects but in the bodies as well. Zim is noted for his detail in his hands and feet.

By 1910 Zim began to publish books independently. His subjects included the art of caricature, humorous histories of Horseheads and Elmira, New York, and tongue-in-cheek philosophies. From his home in Horseheads at 601 Pine Street, he established "Zim's Correspondence School of Cartooning, Comic Art, and Caricature."

During Zim's lifetime, Horseheads' citizens were mostly unaware of the fame of their resident cartoonist. He died on March 26, 1935, and is buried in Maple Grove Cemetery in Horseheads.

A Foolish History of Horseheads lampooned local citizens and local history. There are passages and drawings in this book that may be offensive. Please bear in mind that Zim wrote this book more than one hundred years ago in an area of New York State with no cultural diversity.

More special edition reprinted books from
New York History Review

Zim's Foolish History of Elmira

A Brief History of Chemung County, New York, 1779 -1905

Frederick Douglass' Speech at Elmira, New York 1880

Harper's New York & Erie Railroad Guide Book of 1851

The Elmira Prison Camp

Souvenir of Canandaigua, New York

Erie Railway Tourist 1874

Diary of a Tar Heel Confederate Soldier

Our Own Book : A Victorian Guide To Life

To War and Back - The Lightning Division

NewYorkHistoryReviewBookstore.com

www.ingramcontent.com/pod-product-compliance
Lightning Source LLC
Chambersburg PA
CBHW031602110426
42742CB00036B/665